AF605731

KATE RITCHIE

It's Not SCRIBBLE to me

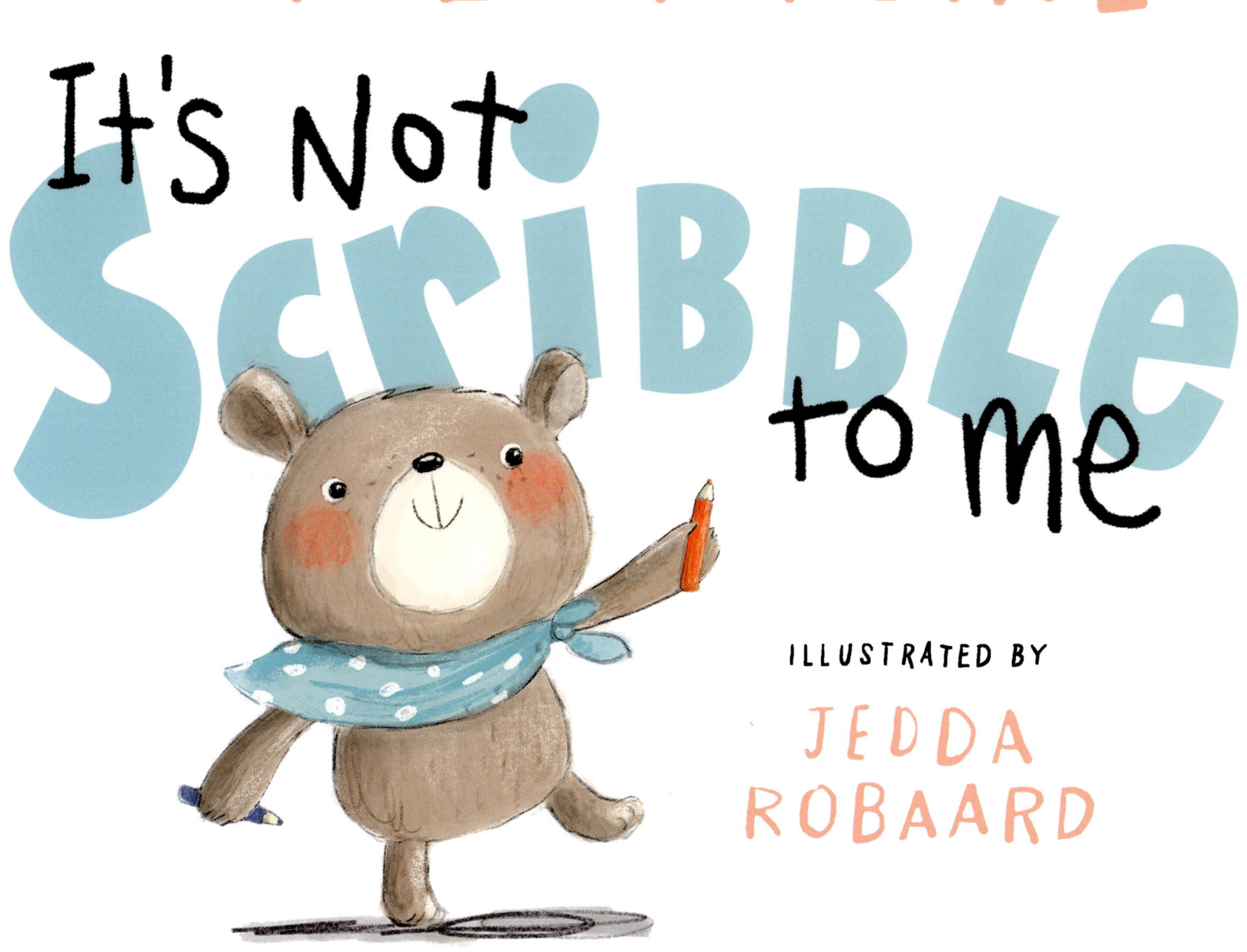

ILLUSTRATED BY

JEDDA ROBAARD

Puffin Books

I have to say I'm not generally bad,
but one thing I do makes my family mad.

I take out my crayons,
my paints
and my pencils –

sometimes the day may call for my stencils.

If I can reach, it's the permanent pens,

then I draw and I draw for hours on end!

Paper is nice but it can't hold them all –

and soon my scribbles spill onto the wall.

You see, Mum, that red is far from a smear,

it's actually Santa, with a grin ear to ear.

That scribble down low that I chose to be green?

It's only a frog, Dad,
not worthy of screams.

The black is a witch,

the blue is the sea,

and the yellow –

you guessed it –

a bumbley bee.

The orange a planet
that's burning so bright,

the purple a unicorn
leaping at night.

The pink on the stairs?

Magic fairy dust showers,

and the rainbow on me
is a big bunch of flowers!

So please, Mum and Dad, the next time you start crying and wailing at my works of art . . .

Take a really deep breath
and imagine you're me,
then look a bit harder,
I promise you'll see –

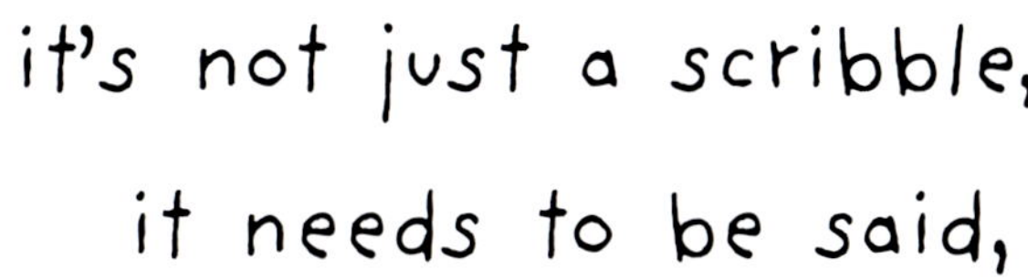

it's not just a scribble,

it needs to be said,

but the
COLOURFUL
MAGICAL
bountiful

beautiful
whimsical
WONDERFUL
world in my Head.

So what about you?
Could you sit next to me,
and please draw me the
magical things that you see?

For Mae. My greatest love and inspiration - KR

For Minnah, my little scribbler - JR

PUFFIN BOOKS

UK | USA | Canada | Ireland | Australia
India | New Zealand | South Africa | China

Penguin Books is part of the Penguin Random House group of companies whose addresses can be found at global.penguinrandomhouse.com.

First published by Penguin Random House Australia Pty Ltd, 2018

Text copyright © Kate Ritchie 2018
Illustrations copyright © Jedda Robaard 2018

The moral right of the author and illustrator has been asserted.

All rights reserved. Without limiting the rights under copyright reserved above, no part of this publication may be reproduced, stored in or introduced into a retrieval system, or transmitted, in any form or by any means (electronic, mechanical, photocopying, recording or otherwise), without the prior written permission of both the copyright owner and the above publisher of this book.

Design by Bruno Herfst © Penguin Random House Australia Pty Ltd
Printed and bound in China

A catalogue record for this book is available from the National Library of Australia

ISBN: 978 0 14379 013 6

penguin.com.au